8 books.

With indices. (Several mispagination references)

Vol 1 pp 36
   2   36
   3   28
   4   32
   5   32
   6   28
   7   33
   8   28

Some leaves fingered and a few minor defects.

Delightful note of ownership on verso of titlepage of Book 4 ×   SJ

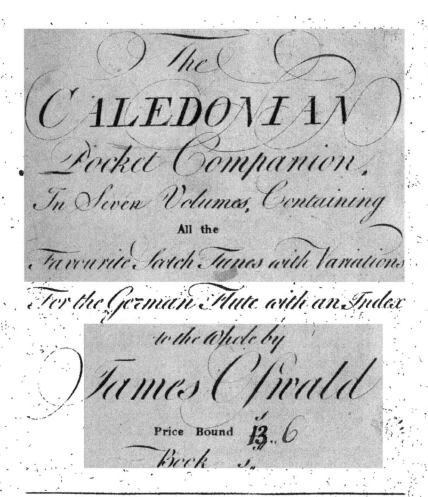

The CALEDONIAN Pocket Companion,

In Seven Volumes, Containing

All the

Favourite Scotch Tunes with Variations

For the German Flute with an Index

to the Whole by

James Oswald

Price Bound 13..6

Book 1.

LONDON Printed for the Author at his Musick Shop on the Pavement St Martins Church Yard, of whom may be had

Just publish'd

OSWALDS Airs, for the Seasons in four Books
The Hessian and Prussian Night Pieces, and Marches
A favourite Book of Duets for two Guitars
Dottels Sonatas and Divertimentis,
Oswalds Scotch tunes for the Harpsicord,

An Alphabetical Index to the 6 Vol.

Vol. 1st

	Page		Page
A Rock & a wi pickle tow	8	The Highland Lafsie	12
Aloway Houfe*	24	The Scots Reclufe*	13
Blink o'er the Burn fweet Betty	19	The bonny Bruchet Lafsie	15
Bonny Mary*	24	To Dauntin me	16
Balow my Boy	25	There are few good Fellows when Jame's awa	20
Cromlets lilt	25		
Drown Drouth	33	The fairy Queen	23
Fife & a' the lands about it	5	The Banks of Forth*	26
Fy on the Wars	7	Tweed Side	28
Failtene Moifq	22	The Bottom of ye Punch Bowl	29
Fy gar rub her o'er wi &c.	32	The Souters of Selkirk	34
Green grows the Rafhes	18	The Highland Laddie	36
Joky blyth & gay	2	Valiant Joky	13
If e'er ye do weil it's a wonder	27	Wally Wally	5
Lord John	25	William & Margaret	9
Love's the Caufe of my &c.	27	When fhe cam ben fhe bohed	14
Mary Scot	4	Will ye go to Flanders	36
My dearie an ye die	10	*Tunes in the 2d Vol.*	
More w Inghean ghiberlan	17	An thou wert my ain thing	16
Maggie Lauder	30	Banquo's Ghoft	6
Nancy's to the Green wood &c	3	Bonny Chrifty	10
Polwart on the Green	6	Bonny Jean	11
Pinkie Houfe	11	Bathra Allan	27
Peggie I muft love thee	31	Blew Bonnet	34
She rofe & let me in	21	Corn Riggs	22
She rofe & let me out	ib	Cumernau'd Houfe	32
She's fweeteft when fhe's naked	26	Come fweet Lafs	33
The Dukes dang o'er my &c.	1	Dumbarton's Drums	1
The Northern Lafs	5	Efke Side*	8
The lovely Lafs of Invernefs*	9	Hamilton Houfe*	6

I love my love in secret	26	The bonny Boatman	28
Jocky's gray Breeches	32	The Shepherds Pipes *	31
Jamie come try me	34	The Cock Laird	33
Lovely Nancy	2	The Mucking of Geordys Byre	35
Lady McDuff's Lament *	4	The low lands of Hollands	36
Lady Macbeath's Dream	ib.d		

Tunes in the 3d Vol.

Leith Wind	18	An the Kirk wou'd lat mebe	13
Lefly's March	36	Auld lang Syne	21
O'er the Muir to Ketty	16	Bonny Dundee	4
Oh, Jenny come down to Jock	31	Bannoks of Bear Meal	6
Peggie's Lament *	29	Befsy Bell	ib.
Strily Vaile *	5	Befsy's Hagges	22
Scoon Houfe *	7	Duncan Gray	8
So merry as we have been	21	Etrick Banks	16
Steer her up & had her gaun	25	For lake of Gold I loft her	2
Sour Plumbs	30	Gilly Cranky	26
The Banks of Tay *	5	Gi'e ye Mawking mair o't	27
The Breas of Birnam *	6	Hei tuti teti	13
The Breas of Ewes *	7	Had awa frae me Donald	17
The Banks of Sligoe *	8	Hallow Een	21
The bonniest Lafs in a' the Warld	9	Joky faid to Jeany	15
		John Hay's bonny Lafsie	20
The yellow hair'd Laddie	12	My Jo Janet	
The gray Ey'd Morning	13	O dear Mother what fhall I do	10
The Lafs of Patties Mill	14		
The Bufh aboon Traquair	17	Sleepy Body	17
The Scots Lament *	19	St Martin's Church Yard *	25
The King fhall enjoy his own again	20	Saw ye not my Peggie	22
		The Mill Mill O	2
The Ragged Sailor	ib.d	Tarry Woo	3
The Birks of Endermay	21	The Lafs of Livingfton	7
Thoro' the Wood Laddie	24	The 14th of October	9
The laft time I came o'er the Muir	ib.d	The Edinburgh Scots Meafure	11
		The Campbells are coming	12

The auld Goodman	15	Miss Lauder	10
There's my Thumb I'll ne'er beguile thee	18	My Apron Dearie	13
		O'er the Water to Charlie	7
The Flowers of Edinburgh	19	Old Collin's Complaint	20
The waking of the Faulds	20	Ofwald's Scots Measure	25
A new Strathspey Reel *	23	Phœbe *	19
D° *	ib	Rofland Castle	3
The Highland Lamentation *	24	Row your Rumple Sauney	28
The Peer of Leith	ib	She griped at the greatest on't	5
The High way to Edinburgh	26	Scots Jig	8
Up & ware them a' Willie	1	The Lady of the Flow'ry Field	4
Woes my Heart that we should funder	5	The Plow Man	6
		The Irish Footman	14
Widow are ye waking	12	The Tears of Scotland *	ib
Wap at the Widow my Laddie	18	The Blossom of the Rasberry	17

Tunes in the 4th Vol.

		The secret Kiss *	23
Anthy the Lovely	8	The Life we love *	27
A bonny Lass to merry me	21	The Maid's Complaint *	30
Allan Water	25	The Lads of Leith	31
A Parcel of Rogues in the Nation	26	'Twas within a Furlong of Edinburgh Town	32
Bonny Lad lay your Pipes down with Variations	18	What shall I do to shoe how &c	1
		Will ye lend me y' Loom Lass	21
By Moonlight on the Green	26	Young Collin is the Pride * of the Plain	9
Cold frosty Morning	16		
Down the burn Davie	18	*Tunes in the 5th Vol.*	
For the sake of some Body	30	Aileen Aroon	21
Good Night & Joy be with you	32	Bonny Kate of Edinburgh	5
If ever I'll merry I'll merry a Wright	12	Bonny Susie *	26
		Cuddy Claw'd her	9
John Anderson my Jo	22	Cheevy Chace	31
I wish that ye were dead &c	24	Daintie Davie	22
If Love's a sweet Passion	29	Dee'l take the Gair &c	23
Katherine Ogie	2		

Farewell my pretty Moggie	8
Faith I defie thee	32
Gilde Roy	20
Hardy Knute	31
Hey my Nannie	8
How can I be sad on my wed.day	12
I cannot win at her &c.	6
I'll never leave thee	14
Jenny & I	27
Jockey & Jenny	31
Ketty's Complaint*	15
Ketty's Scots Measure*	30
Logan Water	18
My Nannie O	3
My Love's in the Broom	ibd
My Dear I dow ne do ne mar	22
My Love is lost to me*	25
Murrays March	27
Norea's Scots Measure*	6
Norea's Lost to me	16
O as I was Kiss'd th'streen	5
Rob shear'd in Her'st	11
Scots Jenny *	7
Sweet's the Lass that loves me	10
There's three good fellows &c.	1
The old Wife beyon the Fire	2
The Breas of Balandine	4
The Glasgow Scots Measure	10
The Shepherds of Yerrow*	12
The Bonny Earl of Murray	13
The Gaberlunzie Man	14
The Aberdeens Scots measure	15
The Colliers Daughter	17
The Black Egle	ibd
The Solitude *	18
The old Jew	19
The Rashes	26
The new way of Wooing	28
The Banks of Severn*	29
Wellcome from Vigo	8
Willie was a wanton Wagg	24
William's Ghost	25
William & Margaret	28
When absent from ye Nymph &c	30

Tunes in the 6 Vol.

Andrew & his Cuttie Gun	4
Annie's Scots Measure*	8
Auld Rob Morris	9
A body Loves me	15
Appie mc Nabb	18
Busk O Busk &c	12
Cease your funning	13
Carle an the King comes	15
Go to Berwick Johnnie	22
Geld him Lasses geld him	23
Gallaway Tom	25
Hossier's Ghost	10
Hit her upon the Bum	17
Hey how the Ballop	20
Iohn come Kiss me now	2
I wish my Love were in a Myre	9
Jenny come tye my Gravat	14
I was not since Martimass	21
My Wife she Dang me	4
My Wife's a wanton wee thing	12
Pattie & Peggie came	6
Sweet Annie fre ye Sea beach	ib
The Old Highland Laddie	1
The Breas of Braukfom	7
The Cyprus Grove*	8
There are few good fellows &c	9
The Broom	21
The Queen of May	24
The Millar of Fife*	ib
The Scots Wriggle	25
The Old Stewarts &c	26
There was a Lad & a Lass	ib
The Happy Night*	27
The Inverness Scots Measure	28
Willie Winkie's Testment	5
What shou'd I do wi an Auld Man	ib
Will you go to Shirriff Muir	10
We'll a' to Kelso go	11
Wallace March	22
I'll never see him more	16

*All the Tunes with this Mark * are originally compos'd by Mr. Osw:d*

An Index to Vol ye 7th

A
At setting Day — 17

B
Burlesque on Black Joak — 18

C
Clout the Caldron — 32

D
Deil Stick the Minister — 30

E
Earl Douglas Lament — 30

F
Fairly shot on her — 28

H
Had I the Wate she bade me — 20
Hey to the Camp — 1

I
Jenny my Blithist Maid — 25
Johnny Cock up thy Beaver — 2
Johnny Faa — 23
Jockey was the Blithist Lad in — 8

L
Low down in the Broom — 6
Lumps of Pudding — 4
Lilli Burlare — 13
Lady Barnards Lament — 24

M
Murland Willie — 11
Mcphesons Farwell — 14
Mount my Baggage — 26
My Love alas is Dead and gone — 33

O
O'er the Muir to Maggie — 16
Old Sir Simon the King — 6
Over ye Hills & far away — 23

P
Pout the Gown upon ye Bushop — 21

R
Ratling Roaring Willie — 9

S
Sailers lead a merry Life — 10
Seaton House — 13

T
The merry Meeting — 5
The Corbey & the Pyett — 6
The Happy Clown — 8
The Old Grey Ey'd Morning — 1
Three Sheep Skins — 10
The Hare in the Corn — 12
Thro the Long Mair I fol- low'd him Home — 30
The Highlanders March — 32
The Auld Maid of Fife — 21
The Milk Maid — 24
The Maid in the Mill — 27
The Scot of Yarrow — 28

U
Up with Aily Aily — 25

W
Where will our good man lay — 22
Wallaces Lament — 7
Walley Honey — 3
Woe is me what Man I do — 15

Index to the 8th Volume.

	Page		Page
Ale Wife and her Barrel	24	Rory Dalls Port	24
Alack and well a Day	27	Robin's Complaint	5
Birks of Abergeldie	16	Saw ye a Laſſie of fifteen	17
Brave Lads of Gallawater	28	Symon Brodie	8
Carron Side	10	Scotch Gavott	10
Currallan's Lament	14	The Bride has a bonny thing	21
Coming thro' the Broom my Jo.	6	The Country Farmer	5
Charles kilt	6	The Widow's Lilt	9
Carlands Devotion	26	The Lee Rig	20
Drimen Duff	12	The Houſe under the Hill	17
Da mihi Manum	16	The weary Pound of Tow	4
Duncans Lilt	14	The Love-Slip	23
Duncans Dance	7	The King of France	26
For the Love of Jean	15	The Vows of endleſs Love	27
Gallaway's Lament	19	The Wars alarms	2
Gentle Love	18	The Royal Lament	2
Green Sleeves	4	The Pangs of Love	15
Here awa Willie	1	Urquharts Scots Meaſure	11
Laſſie with ye yellow Coatie	13	Was ye at the Bridal	7
Maggie's Lamentation	12		
Mc Donough's Lamentation	19		
My Mother ſays I mannot	3		
My Love's a bonny Naithing	3		
Open the Door to three	27		
Omnia vincit Amor	7		
Port Gordon	25		
Peggie of the Green	18		
Port Athol	11		

2

Jocky blythe and Gay

flow

4
Mary Scott
Slow

6. Polwart on the Green

After every two strains repeat the first two

And^te

Brisk

10

My Dearie an ye Die

f low

14

When fhe cam ben fhe bobed

Slow

16

To dauntin me

flow

28

Tweed Side

Slow

30
Magie Lawder
Brisk

Variation

Fy gar rub her o'er with Straw

Slow

36

The Highland Laddie
Slow

Brisk

Will you to Flanders
Slow

The Caledonian Pocket Companion

In Six Volumes, containing all the Favourite Scotch Tunes with their Variations for the German Flute

with an Index to the whole

By

James Oswald

Price bound 10·6. Book 2^d

London Printed for the Author & sold at his Music Shop in St Martin's Church Yard, of whom may be had just published
Six Solos for the German Flute by J. R. Esqr
Eighteen Divertimentis for two Guittars or Mandelins
Gallo & Hasse's Trios — — — — — — — — —
Flores Musicæ being 12 Sonatas by different Authors.

Dumbarton's Drums beat Bonny.

Lovely Nancy by Mr. Ofwald

Slow

The following 10 Airs are scene Tunes for the Tragedy of MACBETH. all composed by M.r Oswald except y.e first.

The Banks of Tay
Slow

Strily Vale
Brisk

Part 2d

Banquo's Ghost

Slow.

Hamilton House

The Bres of Birnam

Slow

Efke Side

Slow

The Banks of Sligoe

Slow

The Bonniest Lafs in a' the Warld.

Part 2d

10
Bonny Christy

Brisk

Giga

Allegro

The Yellow Hair'd Laddie

Slow

Variation

14 The Lafs of Paties Mill

16 An thou wert my ain Thing

Slow

O'er the Moor to Katie

The Bush aboon Traquair

Slow

Part 2d

38 Leith Wynd

22 Corn Riggs

Slow

26 I Love my Love in secret

28   The Bonny Boat Man

Slow

Gigga
Allegro

Pegey's Lament By Mr. Ofwald

Slow

Tak your Auld Cloak about you

Slow

30 Sour Plums

Slow

32   Cumernad Houſe

Jocky's Gray Breeches

Slow

Briſk

The Cock Laird

Come sweet Lass

The Mucking of Geordy's Byre

35

36

The Low Lands of Holand

Slow

Gigg

Brisk

Lafly's March

The CALEDONIAN Pocket Companion

Containing

A favourite Collection of Scotch Tunes, with Variations for the German Flute or Violin

by

James Oswald

Book III.

London Printed for the Author ; sold at his Musick Shop in St Martin's Church-Yard in the Strand

Of whom may be had compos'd for the Temple of APOLLO

Six favourite Songs & Cantata Price — — 2^s
Six Sonatas for two German Flutes by Sig^r Giuseppe St Martini of London, Price — — 5^s
APOLLO's Collection being 12 Duettos for two German Flutes or two Violins all approv'd of, by the Society, Price — — — — — 4^s

Up and ware them a Willie

Brisk

Variation

Bonny Dundee

Slow

Giga

8 Duncan Gray

Brisk

Variation

Da Capo

30. O dear Mother what shall I do

12. The Campbells are comeing

Widow are you wakeing

Aci tuti toti

Mod.ly Slow

And the Kirk would let me be.

Jocky said to Jeany

Brisk

The auld Goodman

Brisk

My Jo Janet

Brisk

Etrick Banks

Slow

There's my Thumb I'll nere beguile you

Slow

Wap at the Widow my Laddie

Mod.y Quick

John Hays bonny Lassie

Slow

The Wawking of the Faulds

Brisk

Hallow Een

Moderately Quick

Var.ⁿ

Auld lang syne

Slow

Var.ⁿ

Bessies Haggies

Slow

Var.

Saw ye my Peggy

Slow

24 The Highland Lamentation

Slow

The Peer of Leith

Slow

Gilly Cranky

Moderato

Gi'e the Mawking mair o't

Moderately Quick

The high way to Edinburgh

The CALEDONIAN Pocket Companion

Containing

A favourite Collection of Scotch Tunes with Variations for the German Flute or Violin

by

James Oswald

Book III

London Printed for the Author & sold at his Musick Shop in St Martin's Church-Yard in the Strand

Of whom may be had compos'd for the Temple of APOLLO

Six favourite Songs & Cantata Price — 2^s
Six Sonatas for two German Flutes by Sig^r Giuseppe St Martini of London, Price — 5^s
APOLLO's Collection being 12 Duettos for two German Flutes or two Violins all approv'd of, by the Society. Price — 4^s

4

What shall I do, to shew how much I love her.

Slow

Brisk

Katherine Ogie

Slow

Brisk

The Lady of the flow'ry Field.

Plaintive

Brisk

Gig

6 The Plowman

Over the water to Charlie

30 *Brisk*

Miss Lawder

My Apron Deary

14

The Irish Footman
Brisk

The Tears of Scotland

Sym.

Cold frostie morning

The Blossom of the Rasberry

Slow

Gig

Brisk

Will ye lend me your Loom Lass

22
John Anderson my Jo.

Slow

I wish that you were dead good man.

Brisk.

26. A parcel of Rogues in the Nation

By Moon light on the Green.

28 Row your Rumple Sauney

Brisk

If Love's a sweet Passion

Slow

For the sake of some-body

The Maid's Complaint

The Lads of Leith

'Twas within a Furlong to Edinburgh

Slow

Good Night & Joy be with you

Brisk

The CALEDONIAN

Pocket Companion

Containing

A favourite Collection of Scotch Tunes with Variations for the German Flute or Violin

by

James Oswald

Book V.th

London Printed for the Author & sold at his Musick Shop in St. Martin's Church Yard in the Strand.

Where is to be had Just Publish'd.

Six Trios by Dottel Figlio	Martini of London's Duetts
Six Devertimenti's by Do	Burneys Duetts
12 Nottumo's by Do	Tessarini's Duetts 2 Books
Gallo's Trios	The Lisbon Minuets
Ofwalds 2 Books of Songs	The Musick in all the Entertainm.ts

Where only is to be Sold the Harp of Æolus
Those that have not the Inventors name on them are Counterfits.

George Bentley
his Book the
Gift of George Bentley late
of Larkstew house at his Decese
he Departed his Life August 1771
and I must keep these Books and
Fiddle for his sake

5

There's three good fellows down in yon Glen

2. The Old Wife beyon the Fire.

Brisk

Fife and all the lands about it

Slow

4. The Brias of Balandine

Bonny Kate of Edinburgh

Slow

O as I was Kiss'd th' Streen

Brisk

Norea's Scots Measure

Brisk

I cannot win at her for her big Belly

Brisk

5

Hey my Nannie
Brisk

Farewell my Pretty Moggie
Slow

Wellcome from Vigo
Brisk

Cuddy claw'd her

Brisk

16 *Sweet's the Lass that loves me*

Slow

The Glasgow Scots Measure

Brisk

Rob Sheard in Herst

12 The Shepherds of Yarrow

Slow

How can I be sad on my Wedding Day

Brisk

The Gaberlunzie Man.

Slow

Kettys Complaint

The Colliers Daughter.

Brisk

The Black Egle

Slow

18 Logan Water

Slow

The Solitude

Slow

Gilli Roy.

Slow

Jig
Brisk

Aileen a roon.

Slow

22 Dainlie Davie. 5

Mod.ly Quick

My dear I dow ne do ne mair

Brifk

Deel take the gair and the Bragrie o'it

Brisk

Willie was a Wanton Wagg.

Slow

28 The Rashes

Slow

Tender, Bonny Susie

Slow

28 The new way of Wooing

Brisk

William and Margret

Slow

The Banks of Severn

Slow

30. When absent from the Nymph I love.

Slow

Ketty's Scots Measure

Brisk

32 Faith I defie thee

Slow

Fine

The CALEDONIAN Pocket Companion

Containing

A favourite Collection of Scotch Tunes with Variations for the German Flute or Violin

by

James Oswald

Book VI.

London Printed for the Author & sold at his Musick Shop in St. Martin's Church Yard in the Strand.

Where is to be had Just Publish'd.

Six Trios by Dottel Figlio
Six Devertimenti's by Do
12 Notturno's by Do
Gallo's Trios
Ofwalds 2 Books of Songs

Martini of London's Duetts
Burneys Duetts
Tefsarini's Duetts 2 Books
The Lisbon Minuets
The Mufick in all the Entertainmts

Where only is to be Sold the Harp of Æolus
Those that have not the Inventors name on them are Counterfits.

The Old Highland Laddie

Brisk

John Come Kiss me Now

Slow

6

4 My Wife She Dang Me

Slow

Gig

Brisk

Andrew and his Cutie Gun

Brisk

Willie Winkie's Testament

Brisk

What shou'd a Lassie do wi an auld Man

Brisk

6

Patie and Peggy

Slow

Brisk

Sweet Annie fra the Sea Beach came

Tender

The Cyprus Grove

Tender

Slow

Annie's Scots Measure

Brisk

Auld Rob Morrice

Slow

I wish my Love were in a Myre

Slow

10 Hosier's Ghost

Tender
Slow

Will you go to Sheriff Muir

Brisk

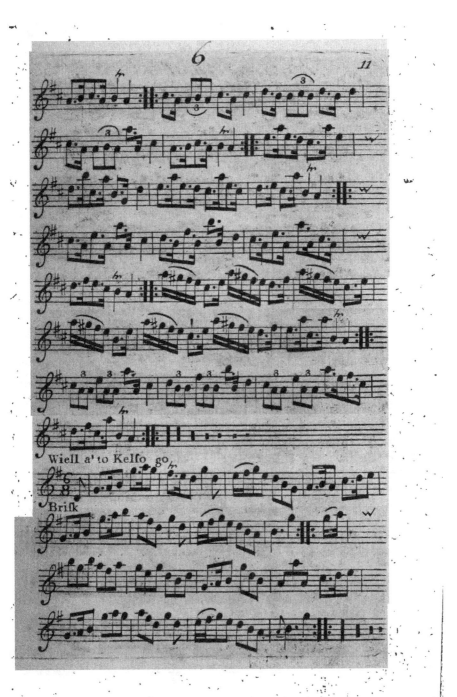

12 Bush O Bush My bonny bonny Bride

Slow

Chor.

My Wife's a Wanton Wee thing

Brisk

14. Jenny Come Tye My Cravat

Mod.ly Quick

16 I'll never see him More

Brisk.

A Body Love's me

Brisk

Hit her upon the Bum

Slow

Slow

Gig
Brisk

20 High how the Bullop

Slow

24 The Queen of May

Slow

The Millar of Fife

Brisk

26 The Old Stewarts back Again

Brisk

There was a Lad and a Lass in a Kilogie

Slow

28 The Inverness Scots Measure

Brisk

FINE

The CALEDONIAN

Pocket Companion,

Containing

A favourite Collection of Scotch Tunes, with Variations for the German Flute, or Violin.

by

James Oswald,

Book VII.

To which is added, a correct Scale for y^e German Flute, with an Index to all the Volumes.

London, Printed for the Author & sold at his Musick Shop in St Martin's Church Yard in the Strand.

THE Caledonian Pocket Companion

Containing

A favourite Collection of Scots Tunes with Variations for the German Flute *or* Violin

By

James Oswald

Book VIII.

LONDON Printed for the Author and sold at his Music Shop in S.t Martin's Church Yard, where may be had just published

Six Concertos in 7 Parts for Violins by M.r Charles Burney	Operas of Demofonte Ripastore Antigono and
Songs in the Burletta forsa padrona	Allesandro with Dances
Six Duets for G. Flutes by M.r Burny	Divertimentis for y.e Guittar
Oswald's Airs for the Seasons	Instructions for the Guittar
Oswald's Solos	Lessons for the G.r by M.r Rush
Marches for the Militia	Comic Tunes in Queen Mab
Flores Musicæ, being 24 Sonatinas for 2 Violins & Violonc.o	Harlequin Ranger, Genii, and Fortunatus with variety of Music printed abroad.

Here awa Willie

Slow

My Mother says, I Mannot

My Loves a Bonny Naithing

4 Green Sleevs

Brisk

The Weary pound of tow

The Country Farmer

Brisk

Robins Complaint

Slow

Symon Brodie

Modertly Quick

The Widow's Lilt

Brisk

10 The Scotts Gavot

Moderato

Carron Side *Plentive*

Port Athol

Slow

Wrquaharts Scotts meafure

Brisk

The Lassie with the yellow Coatie

14 Duncan's Lilt

Brisk

Carrallan's Lament

Slow

16 The Berks of Abergelde

Brisk

Da mihi manum

Slow

Saw ye a Lassie of fifteen Years

Brisk

The House under the Hill

Brisk

18 Peggy of the Green

Brisk

Gentle Love

Slow

Gallaway's Lament

Slow

McDonogh's Lamentation

Slow

20 The Lee Rigg

Slow

Giga

The Bride has a Bonny thing

22 The Ale Wife and her Barrel

Port Gordon
Slow

26 The King of France he run a Race.

Brisk

Garlands Devotion

Slow

28. The Brave Lads of Gallawater

Slow

CPSIA information can be obtained
at www.ICGtesting.com
Printed in the USA
LVHW081140020822
724960LV00004B/92